Sky Magic

POEMS SELECTED BY

LEE BENNETT HOPKINS

ILLUSTRATIONS BY

MARIUSZ STAWARSKI

Dutton Children's Books

To Laura and David Garcia

who brought new magic

to sky

—LBH

To Agnieszka

—MS

Rising

Like a fresh loaf
Sun rises,
Tempting dawn
To break
Her golden crust—

Taste morning!

—Sarah Hansen

Sun

Soleiel!

I'm your star
center stage
the poem on your page
beauty
power
the beat ablaze

I amaze

I am the candle on your cake
a sparkler burning bright

I am light
splendor
bliss

at dawn, your kiss

tenderly
I come to you
a diamond
on the morning dew

I am the wonder of all sky

I am the twinkle
in your eye.

—*Lyn Littlefield Hoopes*

Set, Sun

Time to go
Go down
     now.
Go.
You know
     you cannot stay.
Go down
     now.
Go.
Set yourself.

Take
    the
        breath
            of
               day
                away.

— Lee Bennett Hopkins

Song

Sing to the sun
It will listen
And warm your words
Your joy will rise
Like the sun
And glow
Within you

10

Sing to the moon
It will hear
And soothe your cares
Your fears will set
Like the moon
And fade
Within you.

~ *Ashley Bryan*

11

Who Found the Moon?

Who found the moon?
Who found it when it tumbled from the sky
and picked it up like any common stone
and looked around to see he was alone?
Who licked it with his tongue
to see if it would melt,
and rubbed it with his thumb,
and felt its silver coolness on his palm,
and saw it was no bigger than a plum?

He must have known
that moonlight would be missed.
I wonder if he kissed the moon good-bye
before he wound up knee-high in the grass
and pitched it like a fastball toward the sky—

to hang among the silent stars in space
with finger smudges on its silver face.

— *Alice Schertle*

Moon's Poem

Moon's poem
sings soft,
round sounds of
breezes shushing
through the leaves,
slow rhythms of
spiders swaying,
snails scribbling,
low hushed rhymes
coo-ing
whoo-ing

Each night
Moon writes
a falling-into-dreams poem.

— Ann Whitford Paul

Moon Lullaby

Lull cats to sleep,
let children dream,
shine silver blue
on gentle stream.

Glaze the house
where sleepers sigh . . .
as hours
as nights

as years go by.

—*Rebecca Kai Dotlich*

16

Moon Looks Out

Into the great sweep of silence
Into the limitless space
Into the wide loneliness
One by one stars
Come singing.
       I

          love

             stars.

~Tony Johnston

from

The Rose Tattoo

There is something wild in the air,
no wind, but everything's moving . . .
and I can hear the star-noises. Hear them?
Hear the star noises?

~ *Tennessee Williams*

21

Legends

In the language of stars
lie stories of old
    brilliant legends
    told; retold.

Spelling out sagas,
spilling out light,
    a mythical manuscript

    filling the night.

—Avis Harley

Stars

Connect dots.
Make sky stories.
    Taurus the Bull
    Aries the Ram
    Leo the Lion
    The Big Dipper . . .

Tales stitched onto an endless night.

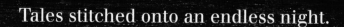

Find a star.
Sing sky songs:

Twinkle, twinkle little star . . .

When you wish upon a star . . .

Melodies sung
in a hushed night.

— Georgia Heard

Orion

Orion in the cold December sky
Looks out upon the earth, the leaves gone by,
Swings over church and steeple down the slack
Of starfields to the western gate our back.
I see his belt (three stars) the studding grace
Of giants striding up through stellar space
Indifferent to satellites and all
That man has made and rocketed. How tall
He stands! How glad I am to know
His name and shape. One wonders here, below
His range and region, why we do not dare
In sight of all the bounty earth can bear,
In loneliness of flesh and blood and bone,
To walk as steadfast, and to walk alone.

—David McCord

Stars

The stars are too many to count.
The stars make sixes and sevens.
The stars tell nothing—and everything.
The stars look scattered.
Stars are so far away they never speak
   when spoken to.

~Carl Sandburg

Last Song

To the Sun
Who has shone
    All day,
To the Moon
Who has gone

    Away,

To the milk-white
Silk-white,
Lily-white Star
A fond goodnight
Wherever you are.

— James Guthrie

DUTTON CHILDREN'S BOOKS

A division of Penguin Young Readers Group

Published by the Penguin Group • Penguin Group (USA) Inc., 375 Hudson Street, New York, New York 10014, U.S.A.
• Penguin Group (Canada), 90 Eglinton Avenue East, Suite 700, Toronto, Ontario M4P 2Y3, Canada (a division of Pearson Penguin Canada Inc.) •
Penguin Books Ltd, 80 Strand, London WC2R 0RL, England • Penguin Ireland, 25 St Stephen's Green, Dublin 2, Ireland (a division of Penguin
Books Ltd) • Penguin Group (Australia), 250 Camberwell Road, Camberwell, Victoria 3124, Australia (a division of Pearson Australia Group Pty Ltd)
• Penguin Books India Pvt Ltd, 11 Community Centre, Panchsheel Park, New Delhi - 110 017, India • Penguin Group (NZ), 67 Apollo Drive,
Rosedale, North Shore 0632, New Zealand (a division of Pearson New Zealand Ltd) • Penguin Books (South Africa) (Pty) Ltd, 24 Sturdee Avenue,
Rosebank, Johannesburg 2196, South Africa • Penguin Books Ltd, Registered Offices: 80 Strand, London WC2R 0RL, England

Compilation copyright © 2009 by Lee Bennett Hopkins   Illustrations copyright © 2009 by Mariusz Stawarski

Published in the United States by Dutton Children's Books, a division of Penguin Young Readers Group
345 Hudson Street, New York, New York 10014
www.penguin.com/youngreaders

Designed by Irene Vandervoort   Manufactured in China   First Edition

ISBN 978-0-525-47862-1

1 3 5 7 9 10 8 6 4 2

Thanks are due to the following to reprint works listed below:

Sarah Hansen for "Rising."
Used by permission of the author, who controls all rights.

Lyn Littlefield Hoopes for "Sun."
Used by permission of the author, who controls all rights.

"Set Sun" by Lee Bennett Hopkins
Copyright © 2009 by Lee Bennett Hopkins.
Reprinted by permission of Curtis Brown, Ltd.

HarperCollins Publishers for "Song" from *Sing to the Sun*
by Ashley Bryan. Copyright © 1992 by Ashley Bryan.
Used by permission of HarperCollins Publishers.

Alice Schertle for "Who Found the Moon?"
Used by permission of the author, who controls all rights.

Ann Whitford Paul for "Moon's Poem,"
Used by permission of the author, who controls all rights.

Curtis Brown, Ltd. for "Moon Lullaby" by Rebecca Kai Dotlich.
Copyright © 2009 by Rebecca Kai Dotlich

Tony Johnston for "Moon Looks Out."
Used by permission of the author, who controls all rights.

New Directions Publishing Corporation for an excerpt from
The Rose Tattoo by Tennessee Williams from *The Theatre of Tennessee
Williams, Volume II*, copyright © 1950 by The University of the South.
Renewed 1978 The University of the South.
Reprinted by permission of New Directions Publishing Corp.

Avis Harley for "Legends."
Used by permission of the author, who controls all rights.

Georgia Heard for "Stars."
Used by permission of the author, who controls all rights.

Little, Brown & Company for "Orion" from
One at a Time by David McCord. Copyright © 1965, 1966 by
David McCord. By permission of Little, Brown & Co., Inc.

Harcourt, Inc. for "Stars" from *Complete Poems of Carl Sandburg*,
copyright © 1970, 1969 by Lilian Steichen Sandburg, Trustee.
Reprinted by permission of Harcourt, Inc.